Wake Up, Dreamer!

E. Chip Owens

DEDICATION

This book is dedicated to my beautiful wife Lillian, who has been a catalyst for me in pursuing my dreams and has been with me through some interesting stages in life. My undying love for you lasts forever and I pray it shows in all I do. You were a Godsend in my life, and you are a miracle each day I wake up. I'm grateful for all that you are and all that you do not just for me, but for our family and ministry. You are the greatest. To my three beautiful children Josiah, David and Zarya: I love you with all my heart and everything I do is to ensure the security of your future. You bring me so much joy and I'm privileged to watch you grow into beautiful people that will one day impact and transform this world.

To my parents, in-loves, and grandparents, you have continued to support me and your cheers and prods are more than appreciated; all that I am is because of the grace of God in you that has been placed in my life. I am because of you. To my God mother, Dr. Lena Warrior, You were one of the strongest women I've ever known and you showed me what it meant to be fearless and go after your dreams. You showed me what it meant to show the authentic love of Christ to people no matter how it made them feel. I appreciate your example and your legacy.

To my transformers, I love you - keep showing the love of Christ by exalting God, equipping other disciples and empowering people to transform and transform their environment. Transformation Church, you are one of the greatest churches on this side of heaven.

To my pastor and spiritual father, Dr. Jamal Bryant, thank you so much for covering me, praying for me and holding me accountable. You are the greatest spiritual father, and I love you for it.

E. Chip Owens

CONTENTS

ACKNOWLEDGMENTS

I would like to acknowledge God for all that he has placed on the inside of me. I acknowledge your dream or vision because it has worth and value to the entire world and I want to see it come to pass. Never despise the process. It is necessary!

Foreword

Warning! Insomnia will be interrupted for every individual with an assignment who has difficulty sleeping. On the anniversary of the million man march the leader of the Nation of Islam, Minister Farrakhan told the masses, "Dr. King wasn't killed because he dreamed, but because he woke up". Chip Owens is on a mission to pull every complacent dreamer out of complacency and into action.

God often uses dreams to get our attention about matters that far exceed our natural comprehension. The images and the metaphors pull us into critical thought so that we must extend what we've known and lean on what we believe. Most people never realize their dreams because they refuse to attach a deadline. Before the concluding chapter you are going to be forced to put some actual work behind what you have seen.

In every dream in the Bible, the person who received was in bed alone. Every now and then the Lord isolates you just to invigorate and inspire. Being alone isn't punishment it's preparation and that's what every page is going to do, prepare you. While dreams do come true, nightmares come a mile a minute for those who don't have confidence in what they conceive.

In 1965 a play entitled "Man of La Mancha" took Broadway by storm and while the plot and story line is now lost on many, the soundtrack still resonates. Peter Otoole sang, "to dream the impossible dream. To fight the unfightable foe. To bear with unbearable sorrow. To run where the brave dare not go." One thing for certain if you really take time to study this book, you will soon discover that your dream is not impossible. BUT if you don't apply its principles you will come to the end of your life sounding like famed fallen rapper Biggie Smalls....it was all a dream!

Introduction

On August 28, 1963, the Rev. Dr. Martin Luther King Jr. stood on the steps of the Lincoln Memorial to deliver one of the most memorable speeches in American history. He was the key speaker for the March On Washington for Jobs and Freedom. This was at a time in America where African Americans and other minorities were fighting for equality and justice. As he looked out onto over 250,000 on-lookers and supporters of civil rights, he began to speak. The first title of his speech was called "Normalcy, Never Again"; however at some point during the speech, Mahalia Jackson, the famed gospel singer, shouted out to this southern Baptist preacher, "Tell them about the Dream!" King had been speaking of a dream for almost three years prior in some form or another, and specifically was referencing the ideological "American Dream" in which minorities were not able to participate due to the privation of rights and the injustices that were so prevalent.

With that prompting, he began to improvise and speak the words that we now know as the "I Have a Dream" speech. In this speech, he began to outline a vision of

America where racial inequality was a thing of the past and where justice was equitable amongst all people. Every individual would be able to enjoy peace and brotherhood based on common humanity, not a society separated by skin color. One aspiration that stemmed from this speech was the idea of being the first minority president. The Dream that King spoke of was the perfect exhortation for men and women of any race or persuasion to rise to the highest office in the land.

Flash forward forty-five years to November 4, 2008: a rising young African American politician, who happened to have just turned two years old twenty- four days prior to the march on Washington, is finally elected to be the president of the United States of America. He would become the first African American to hold this office, and served for two terms for a total of eight years. In that forty-five year span many different things happened throughout the course of American history. Dr. King would be assassinated some four years after making this speech. Many African Americans, after the passage of the voting rights act and other subsequent civil rights legislation, would go on to run for elected offices and some even tried their hand at the presidential office including King's Colleague, Rev. Jesse Jackson, and Ms. Shirley Chisholm.

The Process

Now, for us to look at two historic bookends and negate the actively and struggle, the surrounding factors and climates, that took place in the forty five years in between would be a gross oversimplification. The overarching idea is that there was a Dream, and over time, a person was able to take hold of the office. But in reality, we find that attainment of the Dream required action and as a result of the action the goal was realized. It was not an idea that just materialized one day. It was a process. Though Dr. King was unable to see his dream come into fruition, he worked towards that end until he died, and he mentored those that would continue the work until it was realized. He was an active participant in the fulfillment of his dream.

Many, if not all of us have a dream of some sort. We wish to see something in our lives outside of what we currently see. It could be anything from being a school teacher to a rocket scientist, a preacher to the president. It could be a vision, one of owning a new home, trying to move an organization to a new place, or even being free of student loans. Whatever the case may be, the dream doesn't just come to fruition by itself. Don't expect to be a passive participant and have things happen for you. You must roll up your sleeves, be willing to get dirty and put in the work of going through the process.

When we look at the numerous historical models of dreamers, and going "from a dream to the office," there is no better representation than that of Joseph in the Bible. In the book of Genesis, we find a young man who is favored by his father. His father had two wives and Joseph was the oldest of the favorite wife, so he was special to the father. Not only did he have his father's favor, he was gifted. He was both a dreamer and able to interpret dreams. One day he had a dream and shared it with his family. Like Dr. King, his dream was not followed by an immediate manifestation. He had to go through a process.

One of the most important aspects we must know about our dreams is that they will never manifest if we don't wake up. Dreams can easily turn into nightmares when you choose to not wake up and make the dream come true. Throughout this book we will journey through

Joseph's process, and learn to be active participants in our own dreams.

ॐ

NOW IS THE TIME TO WAKE UP AND MANIFEST

YOUR DREAM!

ॐ

E. Chip Owens

1 DARE TO DREAM

And Joseph dreamed a Dream.... (Genesis 37:4a NRSV)

The Need

The first step in becoming an active participant in your dream is to know that there is a *need* for a dream. So many people have given up on themselves and their potential because they neither dare to dream nor see a need for having a dream, and as a result, they sell themselves and the gifts and talents they possess short. In Joseph's dream, his actions brought about a change in his family's situation: they were already in a good place, but it showed a glimpse of something even better. However, the fulfillment was not intended to be right then; the appointed time would be years later. The dream spoke of things that were to come. The first thing we must do is consider the time table of our dream. Is this something that will happen in a short amount of time or is this something that may be most effective in the future? The timing of the dream will affect everything concerning the plan.

What God has given you is for an appointed time. The world, your community, your home, all of these places are in need of what God is showing you. Your dream is important and needed; it is not just happenstance or a useless fairytale. It is Hope of a better tomorrow. It will not only help you get to your next place, but will be a blessing to someone else and help catapult them to their next place. God is blessing you to be a blessing! Individualistic thinking is the bedrock on which good dreams go to die. When we can think beyond ourselves, the best of who we are, and who God is through us, is able to shine. Your dream will bring provision to someone. Your dream will bring protection to someone. Your dream will bring security to someone. Barbara Sher once said, "Not fulfilling your dreams will be a loss to the world, because the world needs everyone's gift — yours and mine."

Every invention is the answer to some question. The thing that you need to manifest is the answer to someone's problem. There is an incredible need for you to take what is in your mind and spirit and make it a reality. What god has given you is the solution to someone's problem and the answer to someone's question.

Teamwork

Not only is your dream needed, you have to know that you can't do it alone. In the book of Joel, a prophetic word is given that God would pour out His spirit and as a result young men would see visions and old men would dream dreams. The word "dream" used in this passage in its original language of Hebrew was an indication of strength. It was believed that as a boy started to become a man, his transition from childhood to masculinity was marked by nocturnal emissions. If the adolescent had what we now call "wet dreams," it signified him coming into his strength - it meant that he was strong.

For example, in order to determine if King David could remain in the place of being King, the litmus test of his strength was measured by his desire to be with a young woman. He was known for his prowess and desire and when he was not strong enough to perform, those around him knew he was nearing the end of his life. In the Joel text, we find that the old men, those who were entering the stages of frailty and physical weakness, would be strong. How would this be possible? How would they now find new strength?

They would not be doing this alone. The answer is team work.

The text says that old men would dream and young men would see visions. That doesn't mean that they would be doing separate things. It means they would perform separate functions to produce a common goal. The young men are the vigor, strength and continued existence of community. The old men are the advice and wisdom. This is by no means to be looked at in terms of gender exclusivity, because we know that men and women are both vital in every aspect of community. The two, older and younger, together make up the whole of the community and together will help push the dream into reality. The old men don't discourage the young people's visions, they offer the best advice on how to accomplish them based on their past experience.

As elders in the community, they have seen how things happen and know where possible traps, holes and hindrances are. They have seen systems at work and experienced the strategies of those that possibly stand in the way. The young people share the future and the elders give advice on the best practices. You can't have one without the other. It takes everybody.

As a young pastor, it was the voice of my grandfather that helped me most. In my first pastorate, I was a bright, energetic, visionary twenty-eight year old. I was sent by a denomination to a church that had less than five people under the age of forty. As a young man I needed my grandfather who had pastored for fifty years to give me advice and wisdom in how to deal with situations that would arise. He was in a position to give me that wisdom, because he had lived it. He knew what it was like to be a young pastor that had vision. He also knew what it was like to experience resistance and how to maneuver through it. Having both generations is necessary and it leads everyone to success.

Realization

Once you find the emotional esteem to agree there is a need for your Dream, you have to *realize* that you can accomplish it. Joseph realized that even though his situation didn't look like his dream, the dream was possible. He believed in the dream enough that he told people about it. He not only believed it, but he stood behind it. When he experienced opposition, he never stopped dreaming. As a matter of fact, scripture recounts that when he dreamed another dream, he told even more people about it. As he realized his dreams were possible, he put them in the atmosphere. He spoke them, and began to put power and life into the dreams by speaking them. Scripture records in Proverbs 18:21 that "the power of life and death are in your tongue, they that love it shall eat the fruit thereof.[1]" At some point or another you will eat your words. If you keep speaking your dream, you're sure to see it. You have to realize that what God has given you is possible because with God, all things are possible. He has given you something of value, something of worth. God has given it to you for a reason and if he gave it to you it has to come to pass.

On the personal level, one must also have wisdom and zeal. Zeal without wisdom leads to burnout and wisdom without zeal leads to stagnation. Both aspects together lead to achievement and success. In his first campaign, President Obama ran on a slogan that perfectly reflects the attitude of a person that realizes that they can accomplish their dream. When you see the need for your Dream, align your zeal with wisdom, and realize that it can actually happen, then you can repeat to yourself...

---

[1] Proverbs 18:21 NRSV

Yes, **I Can!**

Find Value in your Dream

The coat that Joseph was given symbolized favor and human approval. It was a gift given to him by his father because he was the oldest son of his favorite wife. It was a large price tag so to speak showing that his father placed a high value on his life. The coat is something that he could have lost, messed up, or even had taken. The latter was the case in his story. In order to try a devalue Joseph's dream, his brothers stole and destroyed the coat. Though Joseph never saw the coat again, he never lost his dream.

You need to know that the most valuable thing you possess is not your car, your home, or your wardrobe; it is your dream. You can fall out of favor with people, you can lose your house, you can lose a car, but you can't lose your dream. It's imperative to know that some people may never approve of you as long as you have your dream, you have hope. Helen Keller once said, "Optimism is the faith that leads to achievement…"

Let's Make It Tangible

One thing that will quickly undermine the fulfillment of a vision or a Dream is the failure to make it tangible. It remains in the realm of ideology and rarely gets broken down into practical steps. Vision is for an appointed time and has an objective. One of the most familiar passages of scripture regarding vision can be found in Habakkuk chapter 2, where it says:

> *Then the Lord answered me and said: Write the vision; make it plain on tablets, so that a runner may read it. For there is still a vision for the appointed time; it speaks of the end, and does not lie. If it seems to tarry, wait for it; it will surely come, it will not delay.*[2]

In this scripture, it is clear that the vision is to be written. Prior to the invention of the printing press, which made books widely available to the public, most people were illiterate. Declarations, laws and traditions were passed down orally. Therefore, when someone read something, it was read aloud for everyone to hear. This is why it is said that faith comes by hearing. The word used for run here can also mean "to help." Therefore, the Lord is saying "write the vision and

---

[2] Habakkuk 2:2-3 NRSV

make it plain on tablets so that when it is read aloud, people can help."

The first step in in making your dream tangible is to actually write it all down. This will allow you to actually see the images and words in your hand before you see the full manifestation. You will also be able to rehearse, or "hear," what you want to see. There is power in rehearsing. As I've mentioned before, faith comes by hearing. Authentic faith is putting into action or living out what we say we believe. The more you hear something, the more you believe it. The more you believe it, then the more you will act on it.

It is believed that what many of us have come to think of as a magical phrase, "abracadabra," actually has its roots in the very language Jesus spoke. Its meaning in Aramaic is, "I create what I speak." As you speak a thing you are more energized to manifest what you speak. It is this faith to act that is spoken of in the book of Hebrews that declares "without faith, it is impossible to please God...[3]" Stagnant faith is useless because it won't display anything.

---

[3] Hebrews 11:6 NRSV

9

Hidden in the Habakkuk text are other aspects of vision: resources and purpose. After you have written down your vision, consider and write down the resources you will need to make it work. Those resources could be funds, people, investors, materials, etc. After you have a grasp on your resources, write down 5-10 steps that will help you get from where you are now to what you see on the page.

With all of these steps in place, you'll have targeted points of prayer and faith. Faith without works is dead. Though God is most certainly able to do anything, God most often uses human agency to accomplish things. Therefore, if we choose not to act, we forfeit the opportunity to see God operate through us. This is displeasing to God, but if we focus and operate our faith on what God has placed in us, we will see God work and please him.

One day I talked with my wife and in the course of the conversation I told her something that I told our church later. I told her that in a lot of cases, people have infomercial faith. Many of us have experienced and infomercial in our lifetime. Whether it was because nothing else was on television or not, we've experienced it. The way it works is that a person sits down and watches the infomercial and when they want something, they call and expect it to show up within five to ten business days on the doorstep. This is the same way some people subconsciously look at faith. I can sit by and watch time pass me by and when I see or want something I just pray and ask for it and watch it show up at my door step in five to ten business days. This is not faith and it's not reality. Faith requires action.

This scripture also confirms that we can know that our vision or dream is directly linked to our purpose. Many people go through life wondering what their purpose is. Your purpose is not hard to find. First you need to know that you are uniquely designed by God and fitted perfectly with everything you need to accomplish your vision. Though some of these things may need development, they are already present. With the list you've already created, write down some areas that you are passionate about. They could be education, politics, religion, children, older adults, healthcare, etc. After you write down the areas that you are passionate about, you can take a simple personality quiz and a spiritual gifts quiz. You will see that all of these areas coincide.

After taking these assessments and writing down my passions and vision, I found that my personality, passions, gifting and vision all lined up with being a church planter and educator, and having a passion for social justice. What you were created to do is in you; this is the process of bringing it out in order to accomplish the vision.

YOU HAVE TO REALIZE THAT WHAT GOD HAS GIVEN YOU IS POSSIBLE BECAUSE WITH GOD,

ALL THINGS ARE POSSIBLE

2 DREAM KILLERS

"They said to one another, "Here comes this dreamer. Come now, let us kill him and throw him into one of the pits; then we shall say that a wild animal has devoured him, and we shall see what will become of his dreams." Gen 37:19-20

September 20, 1958: prior to his dream speech, Dr. King experienced an attempt on his life when a deranged woman in Harlem stabbed him in the chest with a letter opener. The woman claimed that she went after Dr. King because he was coming after her. This woman, for whose rights Dr. King and others were so adamantly fighting, felt that the good he was doing was actually intended to harm her! It's amazing how someone's greatness and dream can be a threat to someone else. You need to know that what God has given you is a threat to the agenda of Hell. Before you can even speak it, the enemy will try to destroy it. Your mere presence reminds evil forces that they have no future. Remember, the agenda of Hell and ego is to steal, kill and destroy, but Jesus came to give you a dream and vision that will bring life.

Killer 1: The Dream Opposed

In recent years, a letter surfaced that was written to Dr. King admonishing him to kill himself. The authors of this letter were agents of the FBI. They told King that if he did not kill himself, they would publicly assassinate his character by releasing discrediting information, including proof of his extramarital affairs. The agents threatened to release this information to the entire country, and went as far as to give him 34 days to remove himself from the scene.

Not long after that, on April 4, 1968, Dr. King was assassinated while standing on the balcony of the Lorraine Hotel. A little known fact is that, on December 8, 1999, thirty-one years later, twelve jurors reached a unanimous verdict in Memphis, TN that said Dr. King's assassination was conspired by the government. According to their findings, James Earl Ray, the alleged shooter, was framed and he was not even in the city, let alone the vicinity, of the shooting that day. This suggests to us that the enemy is always conspiring against our dreams and will do whatever he possibly can to kill them.

In the story of Joseph, he had a dream and spoke it to his brothers. He dared to dream and knew that there was a need for a dream and or vision. But, as a result, we find a conspiracy brewing. We need to know that there will always be someone that will try to oppose our dream. The opposition Joseph experienced came from his family members. They were the people closest to him. They were comfortable with Joseph. They were familiar with him. They knew his flaws, they knew his past, and they knew where he came from. They were comfortable with how he fit in their lives. He was the little brother, the youngest son at that time. This dream would upset the norm and they were not comfortable with that. They wanted him to just stay in his place as they saw it.

Oppositions will come from the inside first. The opposition that you initially experience will likely come from people you least expect. These are the people who are the closest to you. They are the ones that are familiar with you. They know your flaws, they know your history, and they know the stock you come from. Part of their disbelief that it's you - they don't believe in the power of God inside of them, so how can you have a great dream or vision when you came from them?

Killer 2: Distraction

Along with the other types of opposition, a dreamer must not be distracted by negative "chatter." In the story, it says the brothers began to talk about Joseph. Before they met with him again, they made a plan. The issue was they didn't like their position in the dream, and because they could not see past it, they tried to destroy the dream all together. One fact about life is that, if you step out in faith, people are going to talk about you. People love back room meetings, telephone conferences, meetings after the meetings, and what I like to call, "heard it through the grapevine ministries". They won't talk in your presence, but will concoct a plan to wreck your dream and you. Most of the time their issues stem from misunderstanding or disliking their place or position in your dream.

If we were to put things in terms of movies, most people want to be the starring role or the lead actor. They don't like supporting roles. They don't like being the one who helps, especially when it comes to being led by someone they think is beneath them, or as in the text, younger. Sadly, many older organizations, including churches, are dying because people cannot see themselves being led by younger leaders. They don't pay attention to the life cycle of the organization and they give little attention to the future of it. But that is a subject for another day.

The funny thing about it is, if people could get past their ego, they could see that they also benefit from your dream. There is a saying that if one eats, we all eat. If your opponents could get past the need for recognition and power they could see that God has an important role for them. In the story, Joseph told them that everyone was represented and present. What am I saying? God could have done it without them. Someone could have been lost or omitted along the way, but whatever God was doing, he wanted them involved.

No matter what his brothers said, it didn't deter Joseph. He kept moving. His dream was more important than their opinions, their conversations, or emotions. No matter what people tell you, keep moving. The objective of a distraction is to get you off course. You need to know that a Dream killer doesn't need to halt you or kill you. They can accomplish the goal of blocking your dream by simply getting you off course. If you can become distracted long enough, you will ultimately never see the dream to fruition. Whatever you do, don't get distracted.

Killer 3: The Dream Aborted

In reality, the greatest opposition and true dream killer is you. The only way the dream dies is if it is aborted. Many times we stand in our own way because we feel inadequate and unworthy. David said "Who am I that you are mindful of me?[4]" You need to know that as a child of God, you are special to God, you are favored by God and you are chosen of God. He has given you a vision, a dream and a purpose for a specific reason that he wants you to accomplish. That business, that invention, that after school program, that service project, that degree, that family member coming back home, being healed, being delivered, whatever God has laid on your heart, it's there for a reason and it's going to happen. I tell my wife all the time, God would not give me what he's given me, the thoughts, ideas, the ability to dream, discernment and taste, for no reason, it all has a part to play in my journey and I'll get to experience the reason. God has given you these things as well. If you

---

[4] Psalm 8:4

can continue moving towards the dream and not act as your own stumbling block, you will see the why and the purpose behind what God has given you.

The Dream Lives On

As we continue through the story, we find that, while others can try to stop it, the dream has a life of its own. The brothers believed that if they killed the dreamer, the dream would be

> **Don't Be Afraid To Fail:**
>
> A quick side bar: don't be afraid to fail. If you have a true passion and drive for success and you don't quite make your goal, it should push you to try harder. I heard a wise man say that the world doesn't pay you for your success, it pays you for your failure, because it's through your failures you show how things work

nullified. They were sure of it, saying sarcastically, "We'll see what becomes of his dreams." What they failed to understand is that, once Joseph spoke it, it was already in the atmosphere. Genesis 37:11 says that Jacob, his father, kept it in his mind. It was in the spirit of Jacob. No matter what happened, Jacob always remembered his son's dream.

The beautiful thing in all of this is, your dream does not have to die. When you speak it, you put it in the atmosphere and somebody is going to catch it. Speak it to someone that is trustworthy and that you believe can help you accomplish it. Avoid people who will either seek to steal it, kill it or destroy it. Somebody is going to remember it. You will experience hardship and opposition, but you have every reason to keep pushing. Never quit! Keep on going! And no devil in hell can stop it from coming forth.

Yes, God Can!

There is a story that many of us heard in our childhood: "The Little Engine That Could". The story took on many forms, but this one started with a little engine sitting in the train yard one day. The engineer came to the engine and told him that today was going to be his big day: he was going to make his first trip on the tracks! In his excitement the little engine began going around the ship yard telling the box cars his exciting news. After a while the big caboose heard this news and said to the engine, "You're too little to pull me. You won't be able to make the trip. You can't do it." Isn't it interesting that when it's time for you to come out of your comfort zone, or when you are about to exit a season, or walk into what God has called you to do, your past and the things behind you begin to speak louder than your future! People begin to bring up your past mistakes and the inner you begins to bring up your past failures and faults.

Back to the story: the engine began to lose confidence, but he quickly remembered two important things that gave him power to overcome all the obstacles. First, the person on the inside of him would give him more power when he needed it, and would steer him in the right direction; and second, when he got to a certain point on the rail lines he didn't have to be connected to the caboose anymore! The boxcars were all set and they began to move. The little engine had just started chugging along when, without warning, they encountered an incline. As they started up, the little engine began feeling the stress and strain of pulling all those boxcars. He got to a point where he felt like giving up. Just then, the caboose started talking (some people would call it honking from the rear), saying, "I told you, you're too small. You're not up to the job and you can't make it."

While the caboose was making all that noise, the little engine suddenly had an inspiration. He could see the engineer, and heard him call his name, giving him instruction and encouragement. At that same moment, the engine felt a surge on the inside. He felt a strength and power that he didn't have before. You see the One that had called him, the One that gave him the vision, had seen the little engine having trouble making it happen. He heard the caboose honking from the rear. And He came to the rescue, throwing coal on the engine's fire. Gradually, the little engine started moving a little faster, and as he did, you could hear him saying, "Yes God can, Yes God can."

As soon as the engine got over that incline, he reached a checkpoint where he was able disconnect from the caboose and leave him there. When he dropped off the caboose, he was easily able to continue his journey. The little engine only had to put up with the added weight and foolish ridicule for a little while, then was able to move on. He was able to *show* the caboose way more than he could ever *tell* him.

You are that engine. You have power inside of you, because greater is he that is in you than he that is in the world. Remember, that while you're on your journey, you get to checkpoints. And at those check points, you can do what the apostle Paul said, and lay aside every weight and sin that gets you off course. If you do, nothing, by any means can harm you. Your dream shall come to pass.

GREATER IS HE THAT IS IN YOU THAN HE THAT IS IN THE WORLD.

3 SOMEBODY'S WATCHING

"He had another dream, and told it to his brothers, saying, "Look, I have had another dream: the sun, the moon, and eleven stars were bowing down to me." But when he told it to his father and to his brothers, his father rebuked him, and said to him, "What kind of dream is this that you have had? Shall we indeed come, I and your mother and your brothers, and bow to the ground before you?" So his brothers were jealous of him, but his father kept the matter in mind." Gen 37:9-11

As a communications major, I had to learn about the history of television. This medium of information allowed for people to visually see life in motion aside from what was actually currently in front of them. By 1960, there were more than 67 million television sets in America. As the civil rights movement raged on, one of the most ingenious ideas that was brought up was to put the movement in the faces of the masses. For the most part, the movement had been confined to the south and the people who were directly affected. By using television, the entire nations attention would be brought to the atrocities that were taking place.

One of the most pivotal moments of the movement came in 1965 when activist marched across the Edmond Pettus bridge in Selma, AL. This was largely in part to the fact that it gained national news attention and people all across the country were able to see what became known as "Bloody Sunday." It was no longer word of mouth conversations about people who had never been seen. It was no in the faces of the masses and those people had to wake up and pay attention. Now things began to change more rapidly because people were watching.

In the story of Joseph we find some interesting things in the person who was watching him. We've discussed how his brothers hated him but the one area that is interesting is the actions of Jacob. We find that Jacob rebukes his son, but the text goes on to say that Jacob keeps this dream in mind. He rebuked Joseph because by saying that his father was going to bow down to the son showed a level of dishonor. In that time the patriarch or the oldest male figure in the family was the authority and by saying that the authoritative figure was going to bow down to a subordinate or a person under them was an insult. Though it was somewhat insulting, Jacob kept what was said in mind.

The reason why Jacob kept this in mind is because it sounded familiar to him. You see in studying the life of Jacob, you will discover that Joseph was almost a spitting image of the positive side of Jacob. In church we spend a lot of time on the trickster side of Jacob, but there was another side to Jacob that warranted God to change his name to "Israel." Israel too was a dreamer, in fact he had a dream where he saw angels ascending and descending a ladder (Gen 28). He then goes on to have an encounter with God that would change his life and the way he walked. Not only that, but he also had struggles with his brother. For Jacob/Israel, looking at Joseph was like looking at himself. It was like watching the part of himself he was most proud of.

He held on to what was said because he knew that there was some merit to what his son saw. He recognized the gift that was work and remembered what God had done in his own life. And if God could work in his life and show him amazing things in his dreams then God could surely be at work in his son's life.

What you need to know is that there are people watching you. They are taking account of your every move. These people recognize the gift on your life and they see your vision. I submit to you that there are people assigned to you your life to help pray you through your process. They may not fully understand everything and they may never put physical assets to your dream, but they are there to cover you in prayer. This asset is just as valuable as a benefactor.

In Joseph's story, his father, the one who represented authority and covering over his life, was able to cover him in prayer throughout his entire process. Though his brothers desired to do him harm and outnumbered their father, they didn't outweigh his authority. So the prayers of the righteous prevailed of the ill will of those who were out to get him. The people that are watching you are praying for you and the prayers of the righteous will continue to outweigh the ill will of any hater you could ever encounter. It does not matter how much opposition you may face.

Not only are people watching, but God is watching. If God gave you this dream and vision, you can be encouraged that God is watching over God's word to perform it. You have more going for you than you do going against you. Not only do you have people and God watching you, but the Bible says that there is a great cloud of witnesses. These are the people that have gone on, your ancestors, the body of Christ that have died, and they are watching you. They are sending their energy to help propel you toward your destination. Your job is to keep progressing and going through the process of accomplishing what God and called you to. By doing this you make them proud, you make those praying for you proud and most importantly, you make God proud. Don't give up, don't quit because somebody's watching you.

.

GOD HAS PEOPLE STRATEGICALLY PLACED, PRAYING
AND WATCHING YOU

4 CAN'T STOP WON'T STOP: IT'S A PROCESS

"When some Midianite traders passed by, they drew Joseph up, lifting him out of the pit, and sold him to the Ishmaelites for twenty pieces of silver. And they took Joseph to Egypt[5]."

As America mourned the loss of Dr. King, something amazing was happening in the course of the dream. The dreamer had been killed, but the dream was still moving forward. Just eight days after Dr. King's assassination, President Johnson signed the Civil Rights Act of 1968, prohibiting discrimination in the sale, rental, and financing of housing. That same year, Shirley Chisholm became the first black female U.S. Representative. A Democrat from New York, she was elected in November and served from 1969 to 1983.

In 1972, the infamous Tuskegee Syphilis experiment ended. Begun in 1932, the U.S. Public Health Service's 40-year experiment on 399 black men in the late stages of syphilis had been described as an experiment that "used

---

[5] Genesis 37:28

human beings as laboratory animals in a long and inefficient study of how long it takes syphilis to kill someone.[6]"

The 1978 Supreme Court case, Regents of the University of California v. Bakke upheld the constitutionality of affirmative action, but imposed limitations on it to ensure that providing greater opportunities for minorities did not come at the expense of the rights of the majority. 1983 saw Guion Bluford Jr. as the first African-American in space. He took off from Kennedy Space Center in Florida on the space shuttle Challenger on August 30.

These were all high points in the fight. African Americans were now able to do great things in society and make history, but then a pivotal incident happened. We found that though we had come a long way, we still had a long way to go.

April 29, 1992: The first race riots in decades erupted in south-central Los Angeles after a jury acquitted four Caucasian police officers for the videotaped beating of

---

[6] Yang, Kaifeng, Gerald J. Miller. Handbook of Research Methods in Public Administration. CRC Press: Boca Raton, FL, 2008

an African-American, Rodney King. As this event unfolded, conceivably, many African Americans feared the fight was lost, but they had to realize: progress is a *process*. As we return to the story of Joseph, we recall that he had had two dreams in which his family was bowing down to him. He told his family about the dreams; they did not like what they were hearing and most of his brothers wanted to kill him. The oldest brother, Reuben, hoping to save him, convinces the others to leave Joseph to die in the wilderness and tell their father a lie. It is at this point that Joseph was thrown into an empty pit. Everything he was experiencing was totally contrary to what God had shown him. I can imagine that, given the circumstances, he wanted to give up and quit, but he didn't because, by God's grace, he understood that obstacles were part of the process.

Have you ever been there? In a place where you wanted to throw in the towel? In a situation that made you want to, in the words of Marvin Gaye, "holler and throw up both your hands?[7]" You thought or saw something good in your future, but what you see now is totally opposite of that and you just want to quit? Don't stop, it's a process!

---

[7] Washington Jr., Grover. Inner City Blues. Kudu. A1, 1971, Vinyl.

The Journey: Will you take it?

The road to full fruition is a journey. After Joseph has the dream and speaks it, the road begins. God rarely gives us the whole picture of how things will happen. He gives us a glimpse and tells us to trust him in it. Your dream will not happen overnight. It will take time and adversity. The journey gives you wisdom to handle the blessing and responsibility you're walking into. Learn the lessons well in order to be a good steward of what God has entrusted you with.

After you <u>realize</u> the dream can be achieved, you have to take on the process of <u>actualizing</u>. It's one thing to say that the dream or vision is possible, but the question becomes, *will you make it happen?* God gives us these dreams and visions, but he also gives us free will. You must determine whether or not you will go after what God desires for you. If you choose to stand and say, "I can and I will do what God has called me to do," it will require you to make a plan, set goals, and sell out to seeing it through.

Importantly, you must know the difference between good ideas and God ideas. Good opportunities will continually appear, but you must stick to your plan. Doing a bunch of good things can get you as far off course as doing something bad. If you chase every good thing that comes up, you run the risk of never achieving your goal. Lao Tzu said, "The journey of a thousand miles begins with one step.[8]" Therefore, it's time to start stepping! But you must always step in the direction of vision.

Confrontation and Reconciliation

Your dream or vision will put you first in confrontation with yourself, and then with others. Joseph was in the pit by himself. In his time of isolation he had to prepare himself for the journey he was about to undertake. He may have had to deal with personal issues. Isolation will put you in a position to where you have to deal with *you*. The time of isolation that you experience should also be a time of preparation - there are things that every person can do to not only better themselves, but to know themselves better. Success can expose flaws, but can also make a person lose sight of who they are and their grounding. Therefore, one should use the time of isolation to ground themselves and become well acquainted with who they really are on the inside, so that when the dream begins to

---

[8] Lao Tzu, "Tao Te Ching," Chapter 64

be fulfilled, they will remain humble, grounded, and able to properly identify areas needing improvement. Isolation is the potting soil for transformation. The model example of this is the caterpillar: it is its time of isolation in the cocoon that allows the process of transformation to take place.

The text says that Joseph was sold to a passing caravan of Midianite and Ishmaelite merchants. The Midianites were the descendants of Midian, the son of Abraham and his 2nd wife Keturah; the name Midian means "strife." The Ishmaelites descended from Abraham and Hagar, Sarah's handmaiden. The last time we see Hagar and Ishmael, Abraham sends them out into the desert after Isaac is born, and we find God telling us at the end of that story that Ishmael's and Isaac's descendants would always be at odds. Two generations later, God's word proved true as the progeny, or "issue" of Abraham, crossed paths again. Your dream and vision will bring you into the company of many people: some people will not look, act or believe like you, but may be people with whom you've had a long connection, and "issues" have come out of the relationship with you or with your family. It's going to require reconciliation.

You need to know that God's dream for you is going to bring you into contact with strife and trouble. That is nothing new: Job said man is but a few days and full of trouble; it's all a part of the process. Before God can allow you to progress into the next phase, you will have to deal with some issues of your past. Every person, no matter how well their life may have gone, needs holistic healing in some shape or form. One cannot healthily deal with other people in a fragmented or injured state. It is said that hurt people hurt people; therefore healing must take place.

There are four facets in the path to holistic healing: remembering, resisting, recovering, and restoring. Remembering is the act of reconnecting with the issue and the stories that were spoken and unspoken. Resisting is getting to a place where you learn to stop going in the same direction or accepting hurt, injustice or mistakes. Recovering is knowing and taking ownership of you: all that you are, all that you're not, right now, without the pretense of "supposed to be." It is the act of trying to construct a holistic self. In this process, you have to recognize your injury, recognize its value and create a space of personal value. The last aspect is restoring. It is resting in feeling good about you, being in a space where you can love and deal with yourself in order to love and deal with others[9].

God's Love = God's Lift!

Joseph's experience suggests to us that, while you will experience some low places, they will not be your final place. For Joseph, the pit wasn't the end; it was only the beginning. Things may have looked far from everything God had shown him, but Joseph continued to trust in God instead of his circumstances. When things seem to be going awry and they don't look like what God has shown you, you have to trust that it's a part of the process. The pits that you will experience will not be your grave, but places to see God's power displayed. They are opportunities to see God show up on your behalf.

Joseph was put in the pit, but he didn't stay there. You can't stay in the low place. You were not called to be a pit dweller, living a sub-standard or sub-par existence. No matter what your pit is: a physical pit, spiritual pit, mental

---

[9] Toure, Itihari. Womanist Ways of Christian Education. Lectures. Interdenominational Theological Center, Atlanta, GA. August- December 2013

pit, emotional pit, relational pit, or financial pit, it doesn't matter. God will pull you out. He wants to take you to your next level. The Ishmaelites didn't just take Joseph anywhere. They took him to Egypt, the richest place on earth at the time. It was the center of learning, wealth, medicine and technological advance. Even though his position was low, he was in the presence of these things. His proximity to greatness eventually gave him access to it.

The hymn writer said,

> I was sinking deep in sin, far from the peaceful shore, Very deeply stained within sinking to rise no more, But the master of the sea heard my dispersing cry, From the waters lifted me, now safe am I. Love lifted me![10]

I know you've heard it before, but I need to tell you again. On this journey, you need reassurance from time to time that God loves you where you are, but he loves you too much to leave you there. God will pull you out.

You can't stop now. God is with you and if God be for you who can be against you? Keep on pushing. Keep on pressing. Make up your mind that you're going make it

---

[10] Rowe, James "Love lifted Me." 1912

happen. Don't let anything stop you. Go for it and see what the end will be. You have a tremendously valuable contribution to make to the world.

ISOLATION IS THE POTTING SOIL FOR TRANSFORMATION.

5 HATERS

But when his brothers saw that their father loved him more than all his brothers, they hated him, and could not speak peaceably to him. Once Joseph had a dream, and when he told it to his brothers, they hated him even more. Genesis 37:4-5

Throughout the narrative of American history, Africans in America have experienced violence in the form of racial hatred. One of the biggest names in racial hatred was and is the Ku Klux Klan. The Ku Klan, with its long history of violence, is the most infamous and oldest of American hate groups. Although black Americans have typically been the Klan's primary target, it also has attacked Jews, immigrants, members of the LGBTQI community, and even Catholics. Over the years since it was formed in December 1865, the Klan has typically seen itself as a Christian organization, although in modern times Klan groups are motivated by a variety of theological and political ideologies.

Started during Reconstruction at the end of the Civil War, the Klan quickly mobilized as a vigilante group to intimidate Southern blacks and any whites who would help them, and to prevent them from enjoying basic civil rights. The Klan's popularity was fed by things such as outlandish titles like Imperial Wizard and Exalted Cyclops, hooded costumes, violent "night rides," and the notion that the group comprised an "invisible empire", which all conferred a type of mystique. Lynching, tar-and-feathering, rapes and other violent attacks on those challenging white supremacy became a hallmark of the Klan.

After a short but violent period, the "first era" Klan disbanded after Jim Crow laws secured the domination of Southern whites. But the Klan enjoyed a huge revival in the 1920s when it opposed mainly Catholic and Jewish immigrants. By 1925, when its followers staged a huge Washington, D.C., march, the Klan had as many as 4 million members and, in some states, considerable political power. But a series of sex scandals, internal battles over power and newspaper exposés quickly reduced its influence.

The Klan arose a third time during the 1960s to oppose the civil rights movement and to preserve segregation in the face of unfavorable court rulings. The Klan's bombings, murders and other attacks took many lives, including four young girls killed while preparing for Sunday services at the 16th Street Baptist Church in Birmingham, Ala.

Since the 1970s the Klan has been greatly weakened by internal conflicts, court cases, a seemingly endless series of splits and government infiltration. While some factions have preserved an openly racist and militant approach, others have tried to enter the mainstream, cloaking their racism as mere "civil rights for whites." Today, the Southern Poverty Law Center estimates that there are between 5,000 and 8,000 Klan members, split among dozens of different organizations that use the Klan name.

After 1968, many of the organized hate groups that we think of splintered off from the massive numbered organizations to smaller pockets. Though the organizational structure of these groups lessened, the crimes committed didn't. Interestingly enough, in researching this sensitive topic, a few other names came up as hate groups, such as the Student Nonviolent Coordinating Committee also known as SNCC, of which Dr. King at one time was leader, and the Black Panther Party. Depending on the author of the narrative the story changes. Only African American authors say that these organizations were organized for the empowerment of the African- American community, not hate, degradation, and violence against other ethnic groups. In the 50 known hate groups in the state of Georgia known to the Southern Law Poverty Center, 6 of them are African American groups. Two are bookstores, one is the New Black Panther Party and three are the Nation of Islam. You can be the judge of that.

Haters are not your enemy

When we speak of a hater, we must define the term. What is a hater? Haters are a tool of the enemy. Most of the time it's not the person that hates you, it's the enemy, operating through them, that hates you. The objective of a hater is to keep you from doing or getting what God says, and the way they do that is by getting you out of position. I Peter 5:8 says *"Be sober, be vigilant for your adversary the devil, as a roaring lion, seeking whom he may devour.[11]"* The enemy is like a lion in that he sits back in the shadows and waits on the right time to pounce on you. He never comes in a straight forward manner. So it is with haters. That's why you have to stay on your guard. Ephesians 6:12: *"For we wrestle not against flesh and blood, but against principalities, against powers, against the rulers of the darkness of this world, against spiritual*

---

[11] 1 Peter 5:8 NRSV

wickedness in high [places].[12]" Your job is to pray for them and continue to do what God says. Haters are *workers* of your enemy. They are not your enemy. Though they are workers of the enemy, God uses them for his purpose.

Haters in your life serve as certification. Certification is defined as attesting something as being true or as represented, or as meeting a standard. Simply put, the presence of haters lets you know that you are meeting God's standard. Trust me, if you weren't doing anything with your life then people would not hate you. If God wasn't working in your life, you wouldn't be met with so much opposition. Haters have a "crab in the bucket" mentality. They see you going higher, and respond by doing whatever it takes to keep you down. They hate out of ignorance: they desire the same blessings you have, but all they see is the glory and not the story. They don't know the things you've been through - and if they knew the half they wouldn't hate again! But, though they form weapons against you, there is no way God will allow them to prosper.

---

[12] Ephesians 6:12 NRSV

Please, don't be naive and think that everyone likes you. You may be the most charismatic, loving person, but everyone is not for you and everyone does not like you. It is not personal though. Sometimes, it is simply the fact that the grace that is on you is intriguing. It is easy to see the great and pleasant parts of your life, but they don't know what you've had to experience to get there. People my age and older can remember life pre-social media. At times I reflect on the fact that in this new day and age, people have become facadists. The idea of the "presented self" is now on steroids and to our detriment at times, we confuse the presented façade with reality. At other times it's not even a façade, its simply the fact that they don't see everything. Whatever the case may be, they like what they see and what it for themselves.

Many times though, our scripture reading gives us a misconception. One of the greatest examples of that is in Psalm 23. We read through the fact that the table is set before us, but negate or overlook the implications of the table being set in the presence of the haters. The implication is this, they are needed and necessary for you to see not only your dream, but the supernatural supply of

God. They also have to be in somewhat of a close proximity. Therefore, you should get happy whenever they get close because it means that God is getting ready to do something.

Friends, on the other hand, are for validation. Validation is defined as support or confirmation of legitimacy. God strategically places these people in your life to support, affirm and reassure you and push you to keep going. Friends encourage you on the journey; they speak life, hope and victory over you and keep you built up in the word.

Watch your back!

In contrast, we find that haters don't talk *to* you, they talk *about* you. Joseph's brothers hated him. When God began using him, their hatred increased. It drove them to act against Joseph, to even want to kill him initially. They would not talk to him, but they talked about him. Joseph was human; he had feelings. It must have hurt to know that those closest to him, his family, the ones he loved and shared life with every day, were the ones plotting against him.

You can expect for people to not be happy when you step out and begin doing what God has called you to do. As a matter of fact, you'd better prepare for it. When people begin to see that God is using you, haters will come out of the wood work. It may even drive them to action. You can expect rumors, lies, ploys, plots and schemes of all kinds to destroy what God is doing, and discredit you. You may be surprised by the ones who are plotting against you. The O'Jays sang, "They smile in your face, all while trying to take your place. You better beware. You know those back stabbers.[13]" Yes, it may hurt, but don't let it stop you.

If your commitment is firm, then instead of hindering your journey, haters can help set it in motion. The actions his brothers took out of hate for Joseph put him in position for the next phase. Had they not put him in the pit he would never have made it to Egypt. His haters set him up for his next place. The actual role of your hater is not to stop you, but to help catapult you to the next level. The bible says that God will make your enemy your footstool. This doesn't mean that you get to walk all over them, but that God will position them to boost you into your destiny.

---

[13] Ojay's. Back stabbers. Philidelphia International A2, 1972, Vinyl.

God takes everything concerning your life and causes it to work out for your good.

They meant it for evil, but God…

Look at the story. They wanted to kill him, but decided to sell him. He was sold as a slave, and he ended up being in charge of a high official's house. He went from being the little brother, to a pit dweller, to a slave, and now he's managing a government estate. He experienced another setback with Potiphar's wife's lies sending him to jail, but that only set him up for more favor. Even though he was in an undesirable position, Joseph still had great success. Grace was on his life. He found favor with God and with people. Though his circumstances were uncomfortable, the most important part in it all was that he stayed on the journey, and God stayed with him.

You, too, are graced for the journey. You may find yourself in undesirable and uncomfortable spots at times, but you can still find success. So look for it. Even though some will hate you, there are those that will be able to see the grace on you. In the words of R&B artist, Jill Scott, "They can hate on you hater, Now or later...[14]" But if you're

---

[14] Scott, Jill. The Real Thing: Words and Sounds Vol. 3: Hidden Beach Track 3,

walking in the favor, grace, love and peace of God, nothing that anyone tries to do to you can pull that off your life. God will open doors that no person can close and close doors nobody can open. Rest assured in the fact that God is with you. Nothing by any means will harm you and you will prosper.

In the last chapter, we looked at the first two steps in becoming an active participant in your dreams and visions. The first is <u>realizing</u> that the dream or vision is possible. The second is making up your mind that you will go through the process of <u>actualizing</u> your dream by committing to make it happen. As we returned to the biblical story, we gained a sense of how these steps are lived out. Joseph illustrates for us that, while going through the process of making the dream happen, some days will be tainted by obstacles and failure; many may not like you, and in fact, some people will hate you. There are some who will simply try to destroy your dream, but there are others who will try to destroy you, your character and your integrity. They will lie on you, scandalize your name and call you everything but a child of God. They, too, serve a

2007, CD

49

purpose in the process. We can't avoid them, but we must be aware of the part they play. Their setback is your set up for your next level. All you need is "bounce back."

For years, I have worked as an elementary school PE coach, as well as pastoring. As a coach, I have access to a lot of equipment, but there was one piece that particularly caught my attention. Out of all the balls I had at my disposal, one little tennis ball caught my eye. There was something different about this ball. All of the other balls are filled with air and, depending on circumstance, if they lose what's inside of them, they lose the ability to bounce back. But the tennis ball doesn't have any air on the inside. You see, the tennis ball is made out rubber. No matter what happens, the rubber will stay consistent. No matter the circumstance, the tennis ball will always bounce back.

No matter what anybody does or says, no matter what plot or scheme is hatched, the grace and favor that is yours means you've got bounce back. When you get lied on, bounce back. When you get mistreated, bounce back. When you get cheated, bounce back. When you get abused, bounce back. When you get scorned, bounce back. When you get talked about, bounce back. It only means you're about to go higher. Remain consistent and watch what happens.

HATERS SERVE A PURPOSE IN THE PROCESS.

6 ON THE OTHER SIDE OF THROUGH-CAPITALIZE

So Pharaoh said to Joseph, "Since God has shown you all this, there is no one so discerning and wise as you. You shall be over my house, and all my people shall order themselves as you command; only with regard to the throne will I be greater than you." And Pharaoh said to Joseph, "See, I have set you over all the land of Egypt." Removing his signet ring from his hand, Pharaoh put it on Joseph's hand; he arrayed him in garments of fine linen, and put a gold chain around his neck. He had him ride in the chariot of his second-in-command; and they cried out in front of him, "Bow the knee!" Thus he set him over all the land of Egypt. Genesis 41:39-43

November 4, 2008: almost forty years after Dr. King's assassination, and forty- five years after releasing his dream for America, something spectacular happened. It was the kind of thing we urged our children to *dream* about, though the average American didn't truly believe it would ever *come* about. If you walked down the street on any given day and picked a random person, they would tell you there was no way - but on that day what seemed to be impossible, what seemed too good to be true, actually *was* true. In the face of underlying racial tensions and against the backdrop of America's jaded past, the first African American president was elected. President Barak Hussein Obama was elected the 47th President of the United States.

We had made great strides as a country: schools were integrated, work places were integrated. African Americans were able to rise to great status in the corporate world, becoming owners of businesses and moguls in their own right. But while these grandchildren and great-grandchildren of slaves were rising to be CEOs and COOs of major corporations, this aspiration had eluded them. The presidency was the one office in the country that had not been occupied by a person of color, though some debate that John Hanson was the first African American president in 1781, under the Articles of Confederation, which predate the Constitution by almost seven years. In any case, no person of color had occupied the Oval Office in the 227 subsequent years of American History. After all this time, and 45 years after King spoke it, we had finally gone from the Dream to the White House.

We were now able to say that the sons and daughters of those persons that built the house had the ability to live in the house. We overcame major obstacles and finally, we reached our goal. Like the infamous scene in "Rocky," we had run and endured the uphill journey and now we stood

in our pinnacle moment with our hands held high. As a
people we sang:

> Stony the road we trod, bitter the chastening rod,
> felt in the days when hope unborn had died. Yet
> with a steady beat, have not our weary feet come to
> the place for which our fathers sighed? We have
> come over a way that with tears has been watered.
> We have come treading our path through the blood
> of the slaughtered, out of the gloomy past - till now
> we stand at last where the white gleam of our bright
> star is cast! For all that we had been through we
> could say that we were on the other side of
> through.[15]

Using the story of Joseph, we've found illustrations of
how to play an active part in achieving our dreams. We've
seen that Joseph had a dream and told his family. To his
surprise, their response was less than positive and he found
himself in a pit. From there he was sold into slavery. While
a slave, he was shown favor. But when his master's wife

---

[15] Johnson, James Weldon. *"Lift Every Voice and Sing." Saint Peter Relates an Incident*. Viking Penguin, 1917

tried to seduce him and he displayed integrity, she was enraged and accused him of assault. Allow me just a moment to say this. No matter what situation you find yourself in, don't lose your integrity! Do what's right and be honest.

Because of this lie, Joseph is thrown in jail, but while there, he is shown favor again. He also meets and works with people who have access to greatness. As a result of these relationships, he gains an audience with the Pharaoh. As we continue to look at the model Joseph presents us, we must draw some conclusions.

You've got to go through.

Joseph had seen the outcome in the dream, but he had to go through the process to make it happen. The dream only revealed the power, not the pain. In it, he saw the prestige, not the passion; he saw the glory, but not the story. He never saw that he'd be sold out, lied on, locked up, forgotten, and that people would turn their backs on him. But everything he went through prepared him for where he was going. Everything he needed for his future he learned in the process - he learned it on his way through.

He learned how to manage and save and be a leader. He gained the wisdom of hardship.

While trying to bring your dream to pass, you're going to have to go through. Everything you need to know for your destination will be learned in the process. The funny thing about God is he'll show you something you're not ready for, then prepare you for it on the way. Duke Ellington once said, "A problem is a chance for you to do your best.[16]" Malcolm X would go on to say, "There is no better than adversity. Every defeat, every heartbreak, every loss, contains its own seed, its own lesson on how to improve your performance the next time.[17]" And Lou Holts said, "Everyone goes through adversity in life, but what matters is what you learn from it.[18]"

My grandfather told me that the things you learn going through the process are sometimes better than the experience of reaching your destination. Don't focus so much on the end goal that you miss the signs and lessons in the process. The things that you experience along the way

---

[16] Ellington, Duke. Music Is My Mistress. De Capo Press. 1973
[17] X, Malcom.
[18] Houltz, Lou

will be invaluable to you and help you in every aspect of your life.

My wife jokes with me a lot about my driving. For some reason, if I go somewhere new in the dark, I learn how to drive there. One thing that has always been interesting to me is that when I drive, I find it hard to stay focused solely on the road. Part of that could be because I'm easily distracted. At any rate, I look and take in everything around my route while the gps guides me, but after I arrive, I don't need it anymore. It is because I learned my way while I was en route. I never learn roads. I find my way by what I see around, the natural features and landmarks. I learn where the potholes are and where the places are to watch.

I am able to learn all of these things, because it intrigues me to see all the things and places I've never been before. The exposure to new places is like images on old film to me. It becomes etched in my brain and no matter what happens, I can almost feel my way back. This is how you need to view your journey. Allow the exposure to things that you've seen before, things you've never felt before and experiences you've never had before be etched into your memory because you will need them again. You will need to use them for yourself and for someone else.

I sat in a service one time and heard the preacher speaking and she kept saying this refrain throughout her message. That refrain stuck with me as a life lesson. She said, "Life is a circle, not a line." Many times we look at life like the dash between two dates on a tombstone, but it is actually more like a spiral. You experience things over and over in different ways and you have to learn the lesson that will allow you to pass life's tests. It is with this in mind that we have to enjoy the journey because if you don't personally see it again, someone will be leaning on you for your wisdom.

Make the most of your opportunities

Joseph shows us that after we <u>realize</u> and <u>actualize</u> your dream, you need to <u>capitalize</u> on opportunities. When Joseph got his opportunity to stand in the presence of Pharaoh, he made the best of it. He didn't know if he'd ever get another chance, so he made a lasting impression. Not only did he interpret Pharaoh's dream, but he offered a solution. God presented Pharaoh with a problem for which only Joseph could supply a solution. The wisdom that informed that solution was gained during his journey.

God will cause an issue to arise for which only you have the answer. When that happens, it's up to you to capitalize on the situation. You have to put your best foot forward, speak up, and deliver what God has placed in you. When God presents you with opportunities, it is crucial to make the best of them because you don't know if you will get another.

One of my favorite movies is "Coming to America." In the movie, there is a scene where Prince Akeem, presents a young lady with an opportunity. A little, old lady on the subway with them says to the girl, "Go ahead honey, take a chance.[19]" That's capitalizing: taking a chance, stepping out and making the move. Realizing allows you to say "I can!" Actualizing allows you to say "I will!" And the result of capitalizing is being able to say "I did!"

The other side

---

[19] *Coming To America,* directed by John Landis, featuring (Eddie Murphy & Arsenio Hall), VHS (Paramount Pictures, 1988).

Be encouraged and know that if you stay faithful through the process, things will change. Joseph didn't remain in the vulnerable and deprived state in which his journey began. Everything he lost in the process, he gained back and more. The story says that he lost his robe, which was his father's covering. He'd had only one, but the text suggests that at the end of the process, he had many. He lost his name and identity when he became a slave. Pharaoh gave him his ring. For the king especially, the signet ring served as both a signature and as a sign of royal authority. In giving Joseph his own ring, Pharaoh bestowed on him rule over the entire kingdom. As one of the youngest sons of his family, he had favor, but no authority. He had a name, but no power. After he went through the process, however, he came out with a name, power and authority.

You need to know that things don't look the same on the other side of through. Everything that you thought you lost in the process will be restored to you. At the end of the course, God will restore the years that the locust destroyed. This is no small feat! In the King James Version of the book of Joel, we find the terms cankerworm, caterpillar and the palmerworm. These are not different insects, they are different stages of the same insect, the desert grasshopper or locust. Locusts in their swarming phase devastate crops. In an agricultural society, that meant that not only was all of their food gone, but also all of their financial resources were depleted, because grain was the currency of exchange. The desert grasshopper also sheds its exoskeleton at least 5 times in the maturation process, and the accumulation of their molted "skin", dead carcasses and waste often preceded pestilence. Equally disturbing, they travel in swarms that can immobilize people as they cover the ground or even blot out the sky.

God will repay

God says in Joel that if his people would turn their hearts to him, he would make up for everything the locust had stolen from them. He would repay them for dealing with the decaying bodies and excrement the locusts left behind. He would repay them for how they were blocked and halted from moving forward.

In the same way, God's promises you he is going to restore the things people have stolen from you. The joy, the peace of mind, the money, the emotional investments, the ideas, and whatever else it may have been. God's going to pay you back for dealing with thin-skinned people that are always offended. They can't take correction, can't take constructive criticism, can't take a complement and can't even receive a greeting of cordiality without becoming vexed. They react to instruction as though you've cursed them out! You'll encounter them along the way, if you haven't already.

God will pay you back for all of the mess you had to walk through. All of the toxic situations, lies and nasty attitudes you had to endure. All of the times people threw you away, turned their backs on you, or dragged your name through the mud. For every illegitimate and untrue scandal that you had to live down, God will repay you for it.

God will pay you back for all of the years of progress you lost. All the time that was wasted in regression, where you felt stuck, bogged down, crippled, and unable to move. For every time you felt pigeon-holed and trapped, every time someone tried to set you up for failure, every ditch that was dug, God will pay you back.

On the other side of this process, God is going to put you into a place of influence. Everything you put your name on, he will make prosper. Joseph's ring and position established him as the second most influential person in a kingdom; before the process, he couldn't even influence the majority of his family. As a result of your diligence in the process, you're going to see the level of your influence increase.

You may have to go through hell and high water, but encourage yourself by saying, "I'm coming out of this better than I went in and I won't look like what I've experienced." You may have been mistreated, abused and scorned, but on the other side of through, you won't look like it. You may have lost a few friends, but you won't look like it. You may have been deprived in every manner of possible along the way, but you won't look like it. Why? Because God used it all to make you better.

Be encouraged! Keep pushing, keep pressing, keep pursuing, and God is going to see you through to the other side. There's a blessing waiting on the other side of through. The process is only temporary. Remember the words of the Apostle Paul that "these momentary, light afflictions don't equal the glory to come.[20]" It will be worth

---

[20] 2 Corinthians 4:17 NRSV

it all, and you can share David's testimony in Psalm 119:71, that "it was good that you were afflicted.[21]"

IN ORDER TO BRING YOUR DREAM TO PASS,
YOU'RE GOING TO HAVE TO GO THROUGH

---

7 Conclusion: There's More to it Than This

But as for you, you meant evil against me; but God meant it for good, in order to bring it about as it is this day, to save many people alive. Now therefore, do not be afraid; I will provide for you and your little ones." And he comforted them and spoke kindly to them. Genesis 50:20-21

O ver the span of this book, we've reviewed several aspects of American history, beginning with Dr. King's Dream speech and culminating with the two terms of President Barack Obama. The thing that's so striking about the election of President Obama is that, while the country was financially at its lowest point since the Great Depression, and against all the odds, he became one of the most successful presidents in the nation's history. Once in the office, he didn't have time to sit back and bask in the glow of being the leader of the free world, he had to work to make sure that the free world remained free. He had to realize that he was a player in a global production.

Something that we all struggle with is transition. One reason for this is that transition makes us uncomfortable; so uncomfortable that we tend to avoid it at all costs, even to our detriment. When we fail to realize that change is necessary and carries a blessing, we focus on its difficulties and lose sight of the bigger picture. This is the final lesson about our dreams and visions that we'll pull from Joseph's story: there's more meaning to the journey than you see right now.

I Am = We Are

We must always keep in mind that we don't experience what we do in life just for our own benefit; we experience it to help others. We are all a part of a greater community. We are pieces of a bigger puzzle. There is an African philosophy the concept of which differs radically from the American or western philosophy of individualism. The philosophy is called Ubuntu. uMunthu (Malawi) says, "I am because we are and we are because I am." It is the belief that we are all a part of a greater community and everything that "I" am, including my identity and resources, is a credit to and part of the makeup of the whole. As a consequence, I have a responsibility to uphold and improve the community and myself. It lends itself towards accountability to the greater society. A person does not live just for the sake of themselves, but for those who have gone on, those they live within community now, and those that will come after.

In the narrative, Joseph could have worried only about himself. After surviving terrible trials and arriving at a place of great status, he could have been selfish and conceited, but his objective was to help others. He protected the nation of Egypt and made sure that everyone was provided for during a difficult season. In addition, he looked out for his family. He made sure that everything they needed, they had. He never forgot who they were or what they did, but he blessed them anyway. To be in a position where he could bless the ones who hurt him was a humbling experience for not only him, but for them as well. The person to whom they did evil was now the one that they had to go to for help. Not only did he help them, but he helped them at no cost.

You are blessed to bless others. Your position in the body of Christ and as Christ's representative in the world is to serve. The hymn writer, Charles Wesley, said "A charge to keep I have, and a God to glorify....[22]" God will place you in a position to be the only one who can provide for the needs of the people who did you wrong. Not only that, the people who tried to knock you down and count you out will have to watch you rise.

---

[22] Wesley, Charles. "A Charge To Keep I Have." 1762

There are some vital steps that should be taken once you have transitioned from your dream to its reality. Honestly, some of these steps should be taken during the process in order for you to be truly successful. First, you need to find a successor. Joseph's story tells us that the older generation places a tangible blessing on the younger. Jacob/Israel, Joseph's father, placed his hands on the heads of Joseph's sons and spoke a blessing over their lives. This was culturally significant, as it was the method by which the birthright was passed down from generation to generation. Along with the blessing came heritable possessions and most importantly the ancestral blessing. This meant approval, well wishes, and confirmation that all through their lives, the God of their ancestors would be present with them.

Pass the baton

When you accomplish your dream, it is important to find someone who will not only keep it going, but take it to the next level. It would be a shame to have a dream or vision, pursue it, accomplish it and then see it die off in your life time. Though Dr. King's Dream was auspicious and the Civil Rights movement saw numerous victories, its effect was not as enduring as it could have been had there been a qualified successor to keep it going after his death. It splintered off into different focuses and factions, and in some ways lost momentum.

My grandfather pastored the same church for fifty years and I was humbled to be able to preach his last pastoral anniversary and retirement celebration. Though extremely well in his health, it was imperative to him that a successor be in place before his official retirement date. He didn't want the congregation to be without a pastor and risk losing any of the momentum that had been created by his success. Mind you now, this eighty-plus year old man is one of the most progressive rural pastors I've ever encountered. Situated in a rural section of north Alabama, the congregation of more than 200 built its current facility under his leadership, and it looks like any urban church in America, replete with TV screens, instruments, a praise and worship team and a new sound system. He wanted to make sure that the church continued in an upward trajectory and made sure that the church had all these things and no debt. When his successor took the helm, he walk in with no church debt and a nice surplus in the bank. In like fashion, once you have achieved a level of success, find someone that will be able to carry it on to the next level and keep your dream alive.

When you find a successor, pass it on. Your wisdom, experience, and authority, properly transferred, will empower the dream and support them on their journey. As I mentioned earlier, I taught Physical Education, and one of our biggest responsibilities each year was preparing for field day. The most popular events were the relay races, with the shuttle relay being the favorite. During the shuttle relay, each runner must hand off the baton to the next runner within a certain zone, usually marked by triangles on the track. In a sprint relay, the runners use what is called a "blind handoff." This is where the second runner stands on a spot and starts running when the first runner hits a visual mark on the track. At the same time, the second runner opens one hand behind them. After a few steps, the first runner should be caught up and able to hand off the baton.

In most cases, the first runner will yell several times. This gives the person receiving the stick the cue to stick out their hand and receive the baton. A team may be disqualified from a relay for losing or dropping the baton, making an improper baton pass, false starting, improperly overtaking another competitor, preventing another competitor from passing, or willfully impeding, improperly crossing the course, or in any other way interfering with another competitor. There is a strategy to how the sprinters are placed. Usually the second fastest person begins the race, the third fastest is the second leg, the slowest is the third leg and the fastest person is the anchor.

On the journey, you have to have faith. Some of the road you will be able to see, but there will be times and instances that are obscured and you'll have to trust your team mates to do their jobs. Most people wish that life had a 360 degree view, but God will give you just enough to get moving. As a matter of fact, you're not supposed to see it all; you're supposed to focus on the vision and run. The vision is the preferred outcome, not the steps to it. Therefore, keep your eyes on the finish line and run for it.

Passing the baton will also require conversation between team mates. You and the person to whom you are handing the baton have to communicate in order for there to be a clean transition. The timing of this is sensitive and critical. If you don't hand off the baton at the right time you run the risk of dropping it. If the predecessor holds on too long, the hand off won't happen correctly and will place you in a position where you may lose. If the person ahead is out of position or doesn't trust his team mate they will also be in position to lose.

How many times have we been disqualified for dropping the baton, not passing it on properly, false starting, getting out of place, interfering with someone else's journey, or not passing it at all and going beyond your leg? It is very possible to threaten the life and vitality of your dream by over running your portion of the race. Transition is a tricky thing, but it is vital to the longevity of the dream. We have to be able to think in terms that are beyond us and the here and now.

The picture is bigger than you think!

As important as it is to pass it on, you have to let God finish it. When it was all said and done, Joseph realized that the journey wasn't finished by him. The attainment of his dream was a work of God's grace. After their father's death, Joseph's brothers thought he was going to harm them. Joseph assured them that he had no desire for revenge. He told them that everything they meant for evil, God turned around for his good and so that others would be saved. Joseph's response came from a place of stepping back and looking at the bigger picture. Even though he had deep feelings about what he had suffered, he humbled himself and saw that there was more to it than that. God had a purpose for what he had gone through. God had a purpose in where he was presently situated. He passed the baton to God and let God finish it.

It is crucial that you know what leg of the race is yours to run so that you can understand how your dream, your vision, fits into the much bigger picture. That bigger picture is God's plan to get people saved. It is God's plan to get people healed. It's God's plan to get people delivered. It's God's plan to set people free. It's God's plan to get people off the streets. It's God's plan to provide care for people.

One thing to note is that the dream or vision that God has given you is just a snapshot in time. If you've ever taken a picture, which I'm sure you have, you know that you can only fit so much in the shot. The picture that you have is only a small bit of the picture and it's just enough for you to handle at the time. It's just a enough to intrigue enough to move and find out what else is there. When go on the journey towards manifestation, you will discover that what God has for you to encounter is beyond what eyes have seen and ears have heard.

It's not your show. It's the Lord's doing. There's another interesting aspect about the relay race. When the runners finish their leg, they don't just sit down and rest, they run alongside and cheer their team mates on. They tell them to keep going and they tell them what to watch out for on the track, because they understand that united we stand and divided we fall. And when you understand that we're all on the same team and we win together or we lose together, you don't have time to tell anybody that they can't do it. Nor do you have time to tell others that they don't matter. You'll push them to be all that they can be.

It is good practice to start being an encourager. A compliment doesn't cost you anything. Make it a point to find at least one person every day to tell them that their gift matters, their life matters and their voice matters. If you happen to be a more seasoned person, you should find a younger person and encourage them to keep pushing, keep pressing, and keep trying to achieve every goal that they have. If you're a younger person, you should find a seasoned person and let them know you are thankful to them for pushing you. Thank them for running their leg of the race and passing the baton off to you. Not only should this intergenerational dialogue occur, but everyone should thank God for being on their team, for giving them a dream, for giving them strength to run and for finishing it up. Remember, he that has begun a good work in you shall finish it.

Les Brown is quoted as saying:

> The graveyard is the richest place on earth, because it is here that you will find all the hopes and dreams that were never fulfilled, the books that were never written, the songs that were never sung, the inventions that were never shared, the cures that were never discovered, all because someone was too afraid to take that first step, keep with the problem, or determine to carry out their dream.[23]

This is the quintessential thought that provokes this entire work If you dream a dream and never wake up to make it happen, it will die with you, and all the potential of

---

[23] Brown, Les.

what you've been given will be buried and lost. It is of the utmost importance that you wake up, throw the sheets back and make the first step. After you take the first step, dare a few more and experience the blessing of what God has empowered you to do.

I told my church one time that if you fail to wake up and achieve your dream, it will become a nightmare that will haunt you for the rest of your days. This is something that I'm all too familiar with. Growing up, I always wanted to be a baseball player. I was actually pretty good at it. I was a little league homerun champion, pitcher, third baseman and so on and so forth. As I entered high school, I tried out for the baseball team in 9th grade. I was brought into a meeting with the assistant principal after the tryouts and he told me that the baseball coach wanted me to drop one of my band classes to be on the varsity team.

I made the worst decision of my life. I made the decision to stay where I was because it was comfortable and because I didn't want to play baseball in the cold. Fast forward about six years and I found myself in a church service. The woman that was preaching, whom I had never seen before or heard of before points to me and begins speaking to me. Her first words were, "I see that you are in the arts, but God said you could have made it professionally in baseball." It didn't help that my new fiancé at the time was standing next to me when she said it. So here this dream is haunting me in my psyche, God is speaking to me and now my fiancé is upset all because I didn't want wake up.

Parts of this story are funny to me when I tell it, but in my mind I still deal with the what if's and regret of "sleeping on" myself, the abilities god gave me and the possibilities that I could have realized. That could have been the answer to the other desire I've had eradicating the mortgage and student loan debt of everyone in my family. That doesn't mean that I'm not going to do that, but it could have been done a lot quicker. Here's is another question to ask yourself, What is easier to deal with, the regret of not doing it or the discomfort of stepping out to do it? Would you rather be uncomfortable for a year or so, or would rather wake up every day for the rest of your life thinking what if?

When you dare to dream, you will run into dream killers. But you can't stop, because it's a process. Once you realize you can make it happen, go through the process to actualize it. When it manifests, capitalize on it. You will be hated, but the good news is that you're still favored. You will come out on the other side of through. Then you will see that the purpose was bigger than the pain. You will be able to say, "I can - I will - I did!" and then, it's time to pass it on.

WAKE UP DREAMER! THE DREAM IS OVER!

GO GET IT DONE!

<u>Critical Questions</u>: Now it's time to write, read, and run!!!!

1. What are you passionate about?

2. What are your spiritual gifts?

3. What is your personality type?

4. What is your dream?

5. Is this something that you are WILLING to pursue?

6. What is the question that you have the answer for? What is the void that you are looking to solve?

7. *The first three questions inform your purpose and what it is,* How does your purpose and dream go mesh?

8. Can you accomplish your dream on your own or do you need help? *If you can do it on your own it's a goal*

9. What are the necessary resources needed to accomplish it? (people, finances, real estate, technology, backing, etc.)

10. Who do you currently know that could fill the need?

11. Is there someone that you could partner with that is already doing what you would like to do?

12. Have you researched what you are trying to do and your needed resources?

13. Who do you need to talk to?

14. What sacrifices are necessary, what sacrifices are you willing to make?

15. Take a moment and reflect, Breathe...

16. Let's work, What is your first step? Many people falter here because they spend too much time worried about step 2,897. Take this step by step and remember it's a journey, not a race. You will get there when it's time.

17. What's step two?

18. What's the next step?

Now that you have all these things on paper, It's time to put your feet on the ground and pursue. The alarm clock is ringing, it's not telling you that you're late. It's telling you to

WAKE UP AND MOVE!

YOU'VE GOT THIS!

E. Chip Owens

ABOUT THE AUTHOR

A highly sought after preacher and author, Pastor E. Chip Owens helps people transform into the highest version of themselves. He draws from his extensive and varied experience as a husband, father, preacher, author and musician to lift and empower his audiences so that they can go on to spread light throughout the world.

A native of Decatur, Alabama, Pastor Owens accepted the divine call to ministry at the tender age of 15, following in the footsteps of his parents and grandfather. Over the last 15 years, he's served in numerous churches throughout the United States, holding a variety of principal roles including Pastor, Minister of Music and Worship Arts and Executive Pastor. Pastor Chip and his wife are the senior leaders of the Transformation Church in Conyers, Georgia, the most powerful place in the East Atlanta metro area, where they love people through the process of transforming the minds and hearts so they can transform the communities around them. They believe in a holistic approach to ministry emphasize that spirituality has an effect on every aspect of the human experience. God has blessed them to experience steady and healthy growth.

Pastor Owens holds a Bachelor's Degree in Communications with an emphasis in Entertainment Media Production from the University of North Alabama and a Master's Degree in Divinity from the Gammon Theological Seminary on the historic campus of the Interdenominational Theological Center in Atlanta, Georgia. The ITC is world renowned for its work in finding faith-based solutions to the challenges confronting the African American community. Pastor Owens will be pursuing Doctoral degrees in both Sociology and Ministry in the near future. A prolific and accomplished writer, Pastor Owens published his first book, 21 Days of Worship: A Devotional for the Worshiper in You, in 2012 to outstanding reviews. He is a member of the NAACP.

Made in the USA
Columbia, SC
27 February 2019